the vertical living room

Joseph A. Little

AuthorHouse™
1663 Liberty Drive, Suite 200
Bloomington, IN 47403
www.authorhouse.com
Phone: 1-800-839-8640

© 2007 Joseph A. Little. All rights reserved.

No part of this book may be reproduced, stored in a retrieval system, or transmitted by any means without the written permission of the author.

First published by AuthorHouse 11/8/2007

ISBN: 978-1-4259-7893-8 (sc)

Printed in the United States of America
Bloomington, Indiana

This book is printed on acid-free paper.

*In memory
of my dear mother,
Wilma J. Little*

*To my father, family, and friends
(natural and spiritual)
with appreciation and love*

*And to everyone who helped
me with this book,
I thank you.*

To every eye that moves upon these pages:

"The Lord bless you and keep you;
The Lord make His face shine upon you,
And be gracious to you;
The Lord lift up His countenance upon you,
And give you peace."

Numbers 6:24-26
New King James

contents

intro xiii

the vertical living room

God's Faithfulness	3
the vertical living room	4
#18	5
morning and evening	6
every morning	8
#14	9

bravo, Lord Jesus, bravo

testimony	13
Hope	15
do you remember	17
The Performance	18
bravo Lord Jesus, bravo	19
and again	20
#33	21
#22	22

now upon a time

the war	25
now upon a time	26
present and future	27
impressions	28
my seed	29
i will not be	30
treasures	31
more than hype	32
awe	33
#46	34

mirror, mirror

the birth of a poet	37
preserved poet, pt. 1	39
preserved POET, pt. 2	43
a poet's rebirth	47
#20	48
what i do have	49
fittin' in	50
mirror, mirror	51
#32	52
fist	53

psalmthesis

revisiting Psalm 119	57
psalm 2005-1	59
psalm 2005-2	60
psalm 2005-3	62
psalm 2005-4	64
psalm 2005-5	65
psalm 2005-6	67

true beauty

#19	71
sister	72
brother	73
crimson aquatic	74
a beautiful journey	75
transforming Presence	76
present tense	77
heavenly	78

the real meaning

you	81

please choose wisely	84
downword/upword	85
the real meaning	87
the telling of secrets	88

Love loves loving

You named it Love	91
gettin' g'd up in Love, ya dig	93
love?.	95
#62	96
the Love Gift	98
just weather Friend	99
Beloved	100
we are gathered here today	101
you may ask us	102
The Messiah Gospel	104

worldwide

mine*d*	107
kings and priests	109
worldwide	113
this is only a test	116
dreamers	117
in october	119
in season	121

support child

support child	125
#48	126
change; ex-currency	127
investment	128
warning, this is a warning:	129
in this moment	130
a healing start	131

selections

the hidden parts	135
Life	137
the Word saving	138
the potential	139
Your peace	141
a thread	143
yes and amen	144
me "church"	147
sunday sounds	149
and you know you should be singing	151
come	152
gifted	154
the Truth is the Truth	155

The Empty Tomb

The Empty Tomb	159

intro

At sixteen, his eyes gazed upon Langston Hughes's "Dreamed Deferred". He had just opened the cover of a book, and there it was, in its own place—its owned place—moving toward him. This poem with white gloves and spit-shined shoes ushered him into a new world, the world of poetry. That same summer, he visited his sister on the campus of Southern Illinois University in Edwardsville, and while hanging out, he walked into the university's bookstore. He was looking for Langston Hughes, and he found him in *Selected Poems of Langston Hughes*. And there between the covers, among the land and the language, the stars and struggles, the love and the lost, he aspired. This poet experienced fire and began writing his own world.

A couple of years later, inside the periodical room of his high school, while working on a term paper, he picked up *Essence* magazine and ran across a poem entitled "Valentines" by Henry Dumas. He felt the poem was a dope way of hipping your lady to all your love. He reread it and then he reread it. Nice. Not fully cognizant of the abundant world of poets, he placed the periodical in its place and continued searching for other articles related to the topic of his English paper, but he always kept Henry Dumas in the back of his mind. It wasn't until his freshman summer orientation at the University of Missouri in Columbia that he met the world of Henry Dumas. Curious to see if the school bookstore had any of his poetry, he searched the aisles just as he did for Hughes, first by subject and then by author. And to his surprise, they did. The book was entitled *Knees of a Natural Man*. Needless to say, he purchased the book. When reading Dumas, the world of poetry was more engaging to him. He was taking root in the land among the trees. He reached up and caressed the brightness of the black and the blue, the tints and shades of all skies, and felt the variations of "how can I tell you how much I dig you, woman." There he was rushing deep like bold waterfalls. This *poet* was introduced to the creative word and the vernacular tongue, the potential and the zenith, the whoa and the shaking of the head. The fire left by Hughes had been given oxygen by Dumas.

There you have it: the natural foundation of this poet; his baptism into the world of nitty-gritty, colorful language. Years came and went. He wrote and he did not write. Time elapsed. He did not pen and he penned. Then, while searching, he was found. Opened were his eyes. This poet had been given a new perspective, a new thought. He was given a new mind. As it is written, so it is: "Therefore if anyone is in Christ, he is a new creation; old things have passed away, behold, all things have become new." (2 Cor. 5:17, NKJ). In seeing, this poet saw the Source of fire and oxygen, the Creator of all things. He saw that faith makes it simple. It is what it is. This is this and that is that. And the truth is there is immeasurable potential in Jesus. He found hope as expressed in "Hope":

> i remember
> the Morning Star
> shining through vast space
> onto me
> and You releasing
> water
> on my desiccated
> essence
>
> and i try to
> multiply You by
> You ...

Multiply. Exalt. Magnify. Celebrate! There are many things in life that people celebrate. It is human nature to celebrate the human spirit, the human journey, the triumphs, the new love—celebrating relationships between human and human, human and world, human and self, human and nature, human and animals, human and things. We read, we observe, we watch, we listen to. Some pay to see; others pry to know who is loving whom or what. We are aware of these things. But there is something quite special about the intimacy of Jesus that should not be held in a bottle or limited to watching from a third perspective. It can be celebrated personally as the poet emoted in "#18":

> ... in Your intentions
> there is eternal goodness
> in Your doing
> it is always the perfect season
> You hear and listen
> and more than anything
> You understand
> You are the Paradise
> of a person, Jesus.

It can be. It is. It is about newness, about the refreshing salvation of Christ. It is a process. The planted. The watering. The growth. The planting. Being loved. Loving. Compassion. Outward. Encouraging. No one should be left behind, discounted, or disregarded. All matters to God: conception, death and everything in between, specifically and addressed by the poet regarding the youth of today and their decisions, as in "this is only a test." But read it a second time. It is a piece for all who are able to procreate. It directs the reader to self-examine before making a major decision. Another poem of the same intent is "mine*d*":

> you have a
>   mine*d*
> of
>   diamonds *are forever*
> within
>   your grasp ...

"mine*d*" starts with words of value, words of worth, words of exhortation. It challenges the hater to stop *hating*. The poem challenges the mislead follower to stop following the un-educated. The poet encourages readers to rock that which God has given them.

Concerned about approaching poetry from Christ-like themes, thoughts of pertinence arose in the poet's mind: poetry is supposed to be relevant; art is to have relevancy. And in most cases, poetry and art do—but God makes it all the more "now-impacting." He makes it all the more "truth-perspective." In presence, in spirit, in flesh, in dying, in burial, in Holy Spirit, He is. In Christ, in temptation, in weeping, in thirst, in answer, in touch, in overcoming, in oppression, in separation, in fasting, in infirmities, Jesus is relevant. He is omniscient. Omnipotent. He is omnipresent. He is omni-omni! Because of this, He can be as relevant in today's prose, facing down today's problems with eternal solutions; can be relevant in today's poet, in you and me, the wordsmith, the storyteller, in your spoken word. Word. World. Your world. Your experience. In life. That is if we allow Him to be. This is exemplified by the Revelation 1:6 themed epic "kings and priests":

> ... men　　　　　　　this is the time
> 　　during milky inhalation and whisky exhalation of
>
> 　　thin new clouds and rusting skies
>
> this is the time for you to let Jesus in your life and
> 　　enlighten you about true love
> 　　　about manhood
> 　　and that you have been called out of
> 　　Elohim's Spirit to be more
> 　　　to be kings and priests.

So note, dear poet, there is relevance here. There is "nowness" within these pages. And note, dear reader, this collection. If you choose not grow roots deep like giant trees, at least sit under them and enjoy their shade, their covering. If you can't lift your arms to caress, lift your voice in celebration, in high, holy, directed praise, and be inspired. Be encouraged, self-encouraged. Be geared toward wise decisions. Receive a seed and give one. Live in Love and sleep away in Love. Accept Jesus.

J. Halal

June 3, 2007

the vertical living room

God's Faithfulness
02.11.2005, 11:00 pm

is as golden ray
    piercing through silver mist
        it is attentive
                to creation
                        as provider
        weaving through
            tender green leaves
        agile
            with the tips of wings
    spiraling gently
    fluttering deeply
            in seas with fins
            and fluorescent beings
        caressing
            the shapes of
                gleaming
            blue lakes
it ascends
    mountain ranges and
    graces
        pinnacles,
    it is intrepid
        with manes of lions
        and an ocean's rage
it is passionate
        about
        all that it touches
    it is
        passionately
            loving to
        all that He has made
            in the earth
and much more
    to you and me.

the vertical living room
11.2006

fertile as
Ancient of
    Days,
 a water of room
        flowing from
            belly
    it glows
of light of
    new day
            outward
descending and
    ascending
are high thoughts
    uniting soul

ascending
    are deep
        verbalizations
to You
    of You
    uniting three-part soul

and come
    visions
            come
              stunning
              vibrant
              visions

now
    go
        write.

#18
02.28.2005, 2:50 p.m.

this morning
You called me
out of sleep
to spend the day with You
just like a friend would
but You are special, Jesus
the perfect Friend
with no pretense
or ulterior motives
in all Your sayings
not one word is against me
but for me
in Your intentions
there is eternal goodness
in Your doing
it is always the perfect season
You hear and listen
and more than anything
You understand
You are the Paradise
of a person, Jesus.

morning and evening
12.26.2004

You
begin
me with You r
unending
loving kindness
    it is
morning
    and to please
You –> i begin:
          asking "how may i?"
so i
    search
Your heart,
    it's center with
the center of
my eye

    i choose to
    please You

and there at the
center
    of You r love
in the
middle
    of You r heart
i find
peace
and it will keep me

all my day

setting now
is the sun
and the moon
      is finding its place
and there
resting in the
      center
of You r heart
      You reveal more
of You r
faithfulness
toward me -
Your undeniable
power
for me
and it is
brilliantly
a-ma-zing.

every morning
01.20.2005, 6:57 p.m.

just the east
most untouched
is glowing with sun
it contains mercies
yet to be experienced
God has some
just for me.

#14
02.28.2005, 11:52 p.m.

there is an
infinite praise
      in my soul
      for You, Jesus

      what You have told me
      weakens me
      in adoration:
anytime that You draw
      me to walk with You
      to talk with You
      is the cool of the day.

bravo, Lord Jesus, bravo

testimony
01.26.2005, 11:00 a.m.

        there was a time when my
     mind was clouded with darkness; heavy.
it was so very, very thick;
       and if my thoughts were sand,
the enemy's footprints were everywhere; and
  sometimes, i didn't know where to
begin; and sometimes, i wanted to
turn back; and sometimes, i did
      turn around; and sometimes i would
  lay in bed and yell "help"
under my breath; and sometimes, the
     tears did run to my pillow-
        case; and sometimes, I couldn't get
any sleep; and sometimes the enemy
had me questioning the questions; and
sometimes, while still breathing, it felt
    like the air was knocked out
of me; and sometimes, i didn't
go to church; and sometimes, when
   i did go to church, i
had contempt; and sometimes, i didn't
    pray; and sometimes i didn't read
   my bible; and sometimes, i just
didn't really know what to do.
     then one day, the grace
    of God came and allowed
    me to say out of my
    mouth, i won't neglect the
    assembly of the saints; i'll
    commit my way to You,
    Lord, no matter what. soul:
    bless the Lord! i said
    bless the Lord oh my
    soul and all that is

within me. and instantly, the
dark cloud disappeared; the burden
lifted; the living water washed
the footprints away. now i'm
truly grateful to the Lord;
and when i think on
that time in my life
and what He did for
me, my tongue remains on
on, thank You, thank You,
thank You, thank You, thank
You, thank You, thank You,
thank You, thank You, thank
You, thank You, thank You,
thank You, thank You, thank
You, thank You, thank You! …

Hope
05.23.2005, 7:09 p.m.

i remember
the Morning Star
shining through vast space
onto me
and You releasing
water
on my desiccated
essence

and i try to
multiply You by
You
not to forget
Light and Life

i remember
You
stimulating
my mind
with liberating caress
and i was
able to form
Your adulations
with my flowing
tongue

it is my hope

and i try to

exponential You
by Your own power
which would
take an endless age

    it is my hope

    Jesus, You are my Hope.

do you remember
07.28.2006, 6:04 p.m.

do you remember
the first time
the Lord proved Himself to you

He was simply dynamic
      so you made love
      to Him with the
      fruit of your lips
      you went on
                  and on
                            and on
making over Him.

do you

do you remember
the first time
the Lord transcended
you out
and He blew
your mind
so much
that He had to
ease up
off you
      not to really wear you out

do you?
do you remember?

He is the same God today
as He was then …

let us look forward to forever.

The Performance
01.25.2005, 10:07 p.m.

stand,
      sit
if you want
      just be still
and know.
           watch Me.

      watch My performance.

that situation
      you seemed to
           have spot-lit,
will become
      My stage,
           My venue.

and if you let Me,
      when I have shown you My skillz,
           that I have tap-danced
                the enemy's
                    back into pieces,
      you will know.

I will say it again:
      when I have showed out
           and displayed to you
      that I am dynamic,
     that I'm the Show Stopper,
           the Headliner
                featuring: ME,
      you will know that
I am
      the only
           Un-com-par-able
           there is!

bravo Lord Jesus, bravo
01.14.2005, 2:01 p.m.

Lord, when i cried out to You,
You stood up for me
Your holy presence covered
the paths of my enemy:
his hold was devastated,
his presence dispersed
my mind was
made clear
when i committed
my way to You,
Lord Jesus,
You showed up
and showed out
Your performance
for me
was nothing short of a miracle
what You did
no one else could attempt
and i run on
and today,
i worship You
i remember You
i celebrate You
i jump in Your joy
i applaud Your greatness
i express words of gratitude
i lose my thoughts in Your glory
Lord, i give You all the praise
Hallelujah!

and again
05.06.2005, 6:28 p.m.

again again again, Lord
again again and again, Lord
Lord, again
again and again
again, Lord, again
again, Lord, You back up
Your word
again You show who You are
You are the Lord of again

wow!

#33
05.01.2005, 11:23 a.m.

JUST LISTEN:
PRAYER WORKS
IN JESUS'S NAME!

JAMES 5:16

- smile -

#22
03.02.2005, 10:07 a.m.

the greatest
most devastating
ceaseless &
victorious
attack on
the enemy
was Jesus's obedience to
the Father
unto death;
He punished the devil.

Jesus is our example.

now upon a time

the war
05.15.2005, 2:25 p.m.

there is a war
of good and evil
happening
before my eyes
it is for my son's spirit
(and he looks just like me)
and this war will
continue
as long as he is breathing

and the angels are vying
for my son's life
so that he won't be turned out
become a crack-head
pimp
or simply
consumed with self
unto a forever death

and because of what i know
can influence the outcome
i have to
tell him daily
about my Lord and Savior
Jesus, the Christ.

now upon a time
05.10.2005, 7:35 p.m.

once upon a time
                in ghetto vernacular
                my father and i had
                condom conversations
                female anatomy talks
                in addition to disease education

i am grown now
and i have my own
and in the tradition of my father
i must talk with my son
while he is yet mine
but our talks
will include that
                which was not between
                my father and i
                though i know he loved me
                dearly
as do i my son
and when i look into his eyes
my words will also include
                an Everlasting Protector
                the One who formed him inside out
                and a Healer

yes
                when i peer into my son's eyes
                while they are yet new
                i must tell him
all that i can
                of Jesus
                and the whole man.

present and future
05.15.2005, 10:40 p.m.

i look at my son
and see myself
and when he says
"daddy"
just as i did
he's asking for answers
he is inquiring
from a pure innocence
about who he really is
and i must tell him
i must tell him
about the fullness of the Lord
because he needs
the right answers
now.

impressions
05.15.2005, 11:02 p.m.

today
i watch him
my lil' man
running and discovering
and, Lord, i don't know how
to be all that he needs
don't really know
where to start
my father was remissive
toward me
but i am alive
getting to know You,
my heavenly Father, and
forgiveness

what do i tell his
impressionable ears
where do i guide his
naissance steps
Father, i know
You are faithful
so please tell me
where to begin
i need Your help …

my seed
07.23.2006, 3:04 p.m.

this living mirror
of clear streamline and
open possibilities
follows me
behind closed doors
me it is capturing
from my groomed head to
dressed toe
from uncut hair to
my bare feet

this mirror living
in my environment
is catching my actions
my entire soul
my will and my emotions
from sunrise to sunset

it is reflecting all of me
and when the time comes
for me to release it
it will be a likeness of
what i did
in daylight and nighttime.

i will not be
07.24.2006, 10:53 p.m.

today
i have made the
decision
i will not be
an enemy
of my son
if i am not for him
i am against him
he must know i love him
and got his back
in word and action
if i don't lead him
someone will
and if i don't teach him
there are many he will learn from
and if i am not around
to speak Life into his life
he will wonder-wander
aimlessly.

i will not be an enemy of my son.

treasures
05.15.2005, 10:03 p.m.

in my hands are precious jewels
of jasper
emerald, sapphire
gifts from the Lord
they are my children
but if i don't
cherish them
enough
to claim them
and proclaim the gospel of Jesus
into their hearing
i have dropped them
and cast them
before wretched beasts.

more than hype
05.28.2005, 2:09 p.m.

if i want my children to see
the mystifying heroism of the Lord
and glorify Him
and imitate Him
as they do superheroes
with their costumes and gadgetries
then i must
do
all i can in order for
signs and wonders
to follow me
i said
when they see signs and wonders
they will
desire to speak life into
dead situations
and see them rise.

awe
05.18.2005, 2:26 p.m.

you should see my children's eyes
light up
when i lean down and
tell them about a mighty God
and all that He has done
One who loves them more than i
and is waiting to show them
only if they would truly
love Him back
yeah, you should
see their eyes
light up
when i lean down and
tell them of Jesus.

#46
05.18.2005, 6:02 p.m.

JUST LISTEN:
IT'S IN THE PRESENTATION
WE MUST MAKE JESUS LOOK GOOD!

PROVERBS 14:25

- smile -

mirror, mirror

the birth of a poet
1991 - 2001

                                       <Henry Dumas>

moon giving way to sun
      blowing cloud white
      waving sky blue
      sliding grass green
      stretching tree brown

    new mercies begin

his curling nostrils catches glimpses of his wife
      and he awakes with a smile—
            ordained love is here

"What ya doin'?" his son asks.

bended knees and raised hands are in his heart
while heartfelt praises arises to the
Lover of his soul

he listens while his Lord speaks ...

more visions are shown
        this is the ultimate Love
and tears swell in his eyes

"What are you making?"

he covers his family with anointed speaking
                    you are blessed coming in and going out.

"What is that in your hand?"

            carrying
            holding
                    the son on his shoulders
his voice trumpets from generation to
                            generation

sun gives rise to moon
        wailing your translucent clouds
        healing our black skies
        speaking their deep grass
        affirming my chocolate trees

molding and molding, he looks at his son and exhales
            "This is the way
            I make
            poems."

preserved poet, pt. 1
01.15 – 02.04.2005

IN THIS TIME
EVENING SHADOWS ARE
HERE
GETTING CRUNKED:

MY EYES ARE NOT BRIGHT
LIKE THEY USED TO BE
AND MILK HAS NOT BEEN ON MY BREATH
SINCE I WAS ABLE TO 21.
STRANGELY, THE
WHITE TOWEL
AT MY FEET
IS STILL DAMP
FROM THE
EIGHTH
POOL.
I HAVE
DISREGARDED IT.

I HAVE BECOME FASCINATED WITH ME:
LIKE
FEEL
SEE.
ANXIOUS
AND
READY.

"WHAT ARE YOU DOING?"
A VOICE ASKS.

I HAVE BEEN
DISCOVERING
NEW
PLACES
FILLED WITH
SMILING PEOPLE.
THE
THIN INTOXICATING
SMOKE LINES
RISES
INTO DIM LIGHTS;
LIGHTS THAT ARE FLASHING
ILLUMINATING
SMILING
PEOPLE.
I KNOW THEM
I CAN RELATE
TO THEIR
EXPERIENCES
THEIR FAMILIAR
EXPRESSION
SOME ARE DANCE SWEATING DANCE
OTHERS ARE CHILLIN'
WITH AGED DRINKS, PROFILIN'
I CAN SMELL
THEIR SCENTS
THEIR FRAGRANCES
I PEEP THEIR

                    CLUB GEAR
                    WE ARE
                    ALL HERE
                    FEELIN' IT.

                    AND WHEN I
                    FINALLY
                    SLEEP TONIGHT
                    I WILL HEAR
                    THE TRUMPETING VOICE
                    BUT I'LL IGNORE IT.
                    I AM GROWN.

    "IS THAT WHAT I THINK YOU'RE DOING?"

                    REVELING.
                    THE FRUIT
                    OF MY EYE
                    HAS FILLED MY BELLY
                    ITS FLESH
          WILL SATISFY ME LONG INTO
                    ROTATING
                    FADING STARS
                    AND THE
                    ASCENSIONS OF
                    RED SUNS
          AND THE FUNNY THING IS
          I'M STILL WON'T BE DONE
                    EVEN WHEN
                    TWO SATURDAYS

MEET.
I KNOW
TO WHERE THIS
PATH LEADS ...

ANYWAY,

I'M YOUNG
GROWN AND
SEEM TO BE
GOOD AT
WHAT IT DO.

"THAT'S NOT HOW I MADE—"

"I KNOW, BUT I'M NOT YOU."

STRETCHING ARE THE
DAY SHADOWS;
THEY ARE STILL HERE.

preserved POET, pt. 2
02.14.2005, 6:36 p.m.

> AMAZINGLY,
> OVER THE HEADS
> OF SHADOWS
> THERE ARE BLESSINGS,
> FULL.
>
> I AM A LITTLE OLDER
> PROBABLY WISER, BUT
> I HAVEN'T REALLY
> CONVINCED MYSELF
> THAT I'M RIGHT
> IN MY CHOICES
>
> I HAVE ALREADY
> COME INTO SOME KNOWLEDGE
>
> BUT
> I AM ENJOYING
> DOING MY THING
> FROM SUNRISE TO SUNSET
>
> AND THERE ARE STILL
> WHISPERS IN MY EAR.
> I AM A DREAMER
> AND SOME
> DREAMS
> BREAK MY REST

                              BUT STILL
                  I AM ONLY YOUNG ONCE
                         AND WHAT I DO,
                                  I DO
                           WHAT IT DO
"I CAN READ YOUR FACE AND KNOW WHAT YOU'RE
THINKING."

                              yes,
            WHAT I AM DOING LEADS
                        TO FIRE
                       the night
                          only
                        facades
                       THE DAY.
            when i can clearly see
                      THAT ALL
                    I ENDEAVOR
                          fails.
            WHAT HAS MY PRINTS
                  seems to fade.
                       DEEP IN,
                   frustration is
                        growing
                     LIKE TREES.
                almost desperate
                  AND FOOLISH:
                       unfolding
               BEFORE MY EYES
                      is failure …
                     DECEIVED.

pale before me are
people
FROM THE
FLASHING
LIGHTS
i touch their
hands
AND MY SKIN
is wet
AND SMEARS AS
MUD

prematurely
(PERIOD)

THERE IS NO
GLORY THERE
when death comes

THIS HAS BEEN
THE ROAD
traveled more.

AND THERE
ARE MORE
DREAMS
and sleepless
nights

     MY SEED IS
     WASTING
      my efforts,
       fruitless
        I AM
      LOOSING
      BATTLES
    and soon the
              war
    I AM TIRED.

"I know the truth;
    I know people have been petitioning for me."

the sun
is shining on
all
that is here
    it is a treasure
    knowing this
    in this age
    while i breathe
    and attempt
to create.

a poet's rebirth
02.14.2005, 4:51 p.m.

the greatest knowing
      that has ever graced my mind
is how much i
      am in need of the
Lord Jesus Christ.

                "Now, this is the way I make poems."

#20
02.28.2005, 5:21 p.m.

me
Jesus

my sin was a river
Your grace is an ocean

my sin was a mound
Your grace is a range of mountains

my sin was a branch
Your grace is the cross

death.
Life.

what i do have
06.01.2005, 2:53 p.m.

today
i have no education
and no job or
prospects of
permanency
but i
have experience d
You
i know what You
can do
and remember
in radical
praise
what You have done
for me

one act
is much
then how much more
are additional acts

today
i have no job
and no education
but i have
experience d
You Lord
and today,
that's enough for me.

fittin' in
08.21.2006, 10:25 p.m.

when i was younger
and discom
fited
i was told:
get in where u
fit
in, foo'.
but now i'm a little older
and realize that
it is a very
danger
      ous
place
fittin' into the world.

mirror, mirror
08.21.2006, 2:06 p.m.

mirror
mirror
do i value this li
                         fe
more than my spirit
                 ual

i don't drink
so i can't drive drunk
i don't smoke to elevate my conscience
  or
        descend
                   to play gangstas-n-ghats
i don't even have unprotected sex
        my bad, i don't have sex, Mom and Pop
and i told you, man, straight-up, i didn't snitch you out

but do i pray
or read the Word
do i even commit to a twenty-four-hour fast
maybe my lips are all over God's names
but where's my heart

mirror
mirror
tomorrow is not promised
so do i value this li
                         fe
more than
my spirit
            ual.

#32
04.12.2005, 7:27 p.m.

i have
two feet
and both feel
left
the right
gear fits wrong
my easiness
eased on
and the drizzling rain
      drops heavy like rocks
            my cool is
confused complication
          which ain't cool, bruh
there is a piece of hair
irritating
the back of my neck
         and i haven't even got a fade yet ...
    my head is up
but my thoughts
are not above
i'm walking forward
but i'm staying in one place
my eyes are open
and there is a piece of hair
in my right eye
         and yo, can i get a Caesar fade
my belly is full
and yet i'm not satisfied
i put my finger on it
but i'm off center.

then Lord, i realize
that i'm missing
the time i spend with You.

fist
07.25.2006, 8:11 p.m.

    for my gift from God, Pastor Matthew Ferguson

it was a time
when i was a
 fist
closed as
arthritis
    tight
    it was truly a
                                           dead
                                                             place

and one day
God's grace
    touched
    me
    to see
the gift
    of my
    pastor

the continuous
    whispering
    of the Holy Spirit:
    he is praying for you

the fierce confirmation:
    you have been on
        my heart and
        my mind

now
i am limber
and loose
 free as opened
       hand

and in regards
       to my
       spiritual father,
i am able
       to receive
       and give.

psalmthesis

revisiting Psalm 119
03.15.2005, 9:09 a.m.

establish You to me for
Your word is You, Lord
Your word
      is You:
on You will i meditate
and contemplate You
in You will i delight myself
You will i not forget

when You open my eyes
i will focus on wondrous
You from You
blessed are those who
walk in You
who keep You
who seek You

Your word is You:

according to You, revitalize me
according to You, fortify me
and grant me You graciously

yes, Truth is
You:
i have chosen You
i have laid You before me
and the course of You i run

in darkness, i remember You
and i keep You
You have become mine
because i kept You

You are a lamp to my feet
and a light to my path

Word up, Lord
and You will draw all men
unto You.

psalm 2005-1
01.04.2005, 8:48 a.m.

Have You conceded Your throne,
    oh Lord?
For there is no other god
    that can follow after You.
No one who can assume Your purpose.
None who can do Your wondrous works,
    Your miraculous acts.
There is no one Abba,
    who can occupy your position.
None can summon the highest creature
    as You Lord;
or whose presence can permeate
    the lowest depths like You.
Lord, i inquire again:
Has Your throne been renounced
    to anyone, anywhere, in any age?
Certainly not, Lord Jesus,
    certainly not.

psalm 2005-2
03.02.2005, 9:27 a.m.

what a priceless privilege
it is to speak of Your
sweet goodness, Lord
it is an undeniable honor
to bless Your name
a great miracle
to possess a thought
a mere inkling of
who You are
You are great
greater than the imagining
mind

sitting above the
circle of the earth
You could have stayed
there in Your might
Your throne of strength
and dominion
and watched
the enemy
have his way
but Jesus, You came down
You came through
as the Source of power
and conquered
his greatest weapon

forever Your throne is established
high above the heavens
surpassing undiscovered
galaxies
and unreachable
sources of light
Your throne is the beginning
of unnamed stars and planets
and the end of obscure distances

You are awesome,
just awesome.

psalm 2005-3
01.07.2005

I have not changed
Who am I?
if the sun were to melt in
an ocean of My consuming fire
and the moon were to dissolve
into dust,
can't I form multiple sets?
don't dwell on the sky
when I am the Lord who knows
they are missing
why would you look to their
places when I am positioned high
above them?
magnify Me
through all times
look to Me
through every situation
focus on Me,
for I am able to be a moon that
out glow any sun
and those things being natural
then how much more
spiritual, for I am the
Lord of spirits!
meditate on Me
don't forget Me
don't forget what I have done for you
I can perform them again
I am the same
I have not changed
I am able to lift every burden and
give you unquenchable joy
I am able to crack the enemy's back
and destruct his every plan

I am your salvation
turn to Me
keep Me and let all else go
I am your way of deliverance
meditate on Me
I am   your way   of deliverance
I am the same
I have not changed.

psalm 2005-4
01.05.2005, 6:30 p.m.

in my
emptiness
i long for Your strength
in my decreasing,
i cry for Your comforting presence
oh Lord, manifest more of
Your strength to me,
for when i am weak, it is
perfected.

what can i be without You,
what will i become?
from what direction will
my help emerge, if You are
not its source.

it is You i search for,
for without You, i go against
Your will.

to You i run,
for it is You who comforts
it is You who truly helps -
who rescues me
it is You
who truly fills
it is You
who hears my cry
it is You, oh Lord,
it is You.

psalm 2005-5
03.15.2005, 9:52 a.m.

when i open You word
dimensions
are present
      as living
           pop-up books

and turning pages
a new world
is shown to me

simplicity

i can see the seed
in the apple
of a tree
in the midst
of the orchard
      there are acres
           rolling forever

i can peer
into the neutron
in the center
of the sun
and watch
energy be released

my mind is open
and blank
like a canvas for
Your painting, Lord Jesus:
tigers are pursuing through
the hairs of Your brow,
in abundance are cardinals

perching the quietness
of Your palms
i see
gazelles leaping the
broadness of Your chest
and butterflies break free at
Your nape

You are Creator.

and yes, Your children feed
at the crests of Your lips:

Your word is living
       bread …

i open Your word
and it is
dimensionally
alive, Lord!

psalm 2005-6
02.22.2005

covering transgressions
I left a circle of worship
a glorious place of exaltation for you
I became humble
lowering Myself
with transgressors for you
                    to cover you
                    your filthiness
                    your shame

                    covering the Transgression
                    of mankind
seeking to be loved
        adored
        as only as I can
by you ...

true beauty

#19
02.28.2005

there is a beauty
beyond imagination
whose roots flourish
in worship
it is attractive
a sweet nectar
of delight
and whole
the purpose pleasure of worship
the choice to do
and the consequence of doing

peace

neither worlds
can taint it

it is flawless
beyond comparison
acknowledging the Lord's greatness
it is so ceaseless
and quite unattainable
but accessible
in Truth to
those He calls His own.

sister
03.13.2005, 9:51 p.m.

    for W.L.G.

her heart is bowing
in the intensity of His love
God is loving her
He is spiraling around her
like sweet wind
ascending and descending
on her
from numbered hair
to precious toes
He is moving through her,
altogether,
gently
from the center
of her spirit
to the lining of her lips
not being able to articulate
the greatness that is filling
her mind
she shakes her weeping head
the Lord is loving her
and anything
created
cannot
stop Him.

brother
05.15.2005, 1:53 p.m.

for D.B.

Lord, You have touched my lil' brother
in a place
that has set his spirit on fire
You have impressed him
and Your print is all over
his heart
and it burns
to the uplifting
of his hands
he praises You fully
and he worships You openly
so that it blesses those
who know You
Your experience
it is love they are watching
he is adoring You,
what they are hearing

it is love being made.

crimson aquatic
05.02.2005, 10:09 p.m.

the Lord's heart is calling
calling
calling me
it is an incessant fountain of
an aquatic crimson redemption
drawing me nearer to Him
inward;
come
and dive deep.

a beautiful journey
01.04.2005, 10:08 a.m.

on a beautiful journey
You lead me:
Your will
becomes my total desire,
my complete heart
flourishes into Your word
in Your presence
i am tender and
open
to Your voice
i am exposed to
Your sound
i am moving in
Your radiant Spirit
i am breathing Life
Your character is
as refreshing as
breezes
 in summer
i am tasting You, Lord
and delighted
i am catching glimpses
of You
and is in awe
for on this beautiful journey
    where heart blooms
    into Your word
    and desire conforms
    to Your will
i am being perfected for
Your everlasting pleasure.

transforming Presence
01.11.2005, 6:41 p.m.

here Holy Spirit
as streaming blue water hills
Your image i'll be.

present tense
01.24.2005, 9:33 a.m.

    Holy Spirit,
        i am feeling Your love.
        i am being outdone.
        i am being worn out by Your feeling.
        i am weeping like a child.
        i am being renewed.
    right now,
i am being changed.

heavenly
01.18.2005, 2:13 p.m.

     when You come,
Holy Spirit,
my language,
like fervent air,
rises and transforms
into heavenly words

and the things i say
and the things i speak   are heavenly.

i say
     when You come,
Holy Spirit,
like winter air
my thoughts
are clearly pure and renewed

and the things i think on
and the things i meditate on are just heavenly.

the real meaning

you
summer 2002

a few days ago:
you
young and fresh
vibrant and full
quick and open
new
you
amazed and smiling
wondering and inquiring
thinking and aspiring
determined
moving
you

today:
you
older and tired
dry and bare
slow and shutdown
you
trick   ed
deceived
you
played
touched and spoiled
complex and broke
questioning and sad
stag   nated
you

somewhere in between
them days:
you
heard words
you
listened to words
believed those words
cursed by those words
you
unprotected
uncovered
un-positively
uprooted
you
lived those words
lived in those words
dying because of those words
you
didn't know
no better

but now
right now
the Word
is nigh
and you
can live
can
rise up
be blessed

you
again.
you
again:
can live
Life
in Word
healed and whole

you

and don't
you
forget it!

please choose wisely
summer 2002

today, words
full
of power   like dark skies without gleam nor ray
nor break are moving and they are
empty and void   they are
deprived and wanting
in them   there is
no promise nor prolific visions—only death.
    right now, echoes of deceptions and accusations
travel
the air.

today, words full of
power   like living rivers from a new
spring are flowing. they are
rushing to thirsty lands   they are
wise and rich   they are
seeking   [searching minds] to nurture—to enlighten
    right now, voices are speaking the truth reality
into
the spirit.

today, the choice is yours
    to speak the power of dark skies or living rivers

please, choose wisely.

downword/upword
summer 2002

behind
the uplifted spirit and the wounded soul
i am there
at the mouth of
      law and punishment
      shepherds and flocks
      discord and harmony
i am right there
i am present
      influencing
      affecting
i am in marches, at protests and sit-ins

                i was at Selma, Montgomery, and D.C.
                      at Columbine and L.A.

                      i was at the slave auctions
and
      is in the voting booths ...

                riding at the back of the bus and
                flying in aimed airplanes   i was there

i am in the church
      with your sin or your sacrifice
i am on the corner
at the hospital

between sheets and
in the grave

        i was (**am?**) at the root of strange fruit
and in the seed of your heart
i am in your son's mind
and your daughter's ear
i'm in the smile and the tear

i have given life and death

right now, i am at the tip of your tongue.

i am the power of words
    your words.

the real meaning
01.29.2005, 12:41 p.m.

    intent is bursting
        the seams of
      the *li* and the *ke*
    the *lo* and the *ve*
      even when the *lu* and the *st*
          are at
         the tips of
         your fingers.

    from the capital to the period
      clandestine reasons
        open the mouths
   in moments
       pervaded with
         self-passions

       don't be deceived
     the vain ones will be
         accounted for
  check the heart
       let us check our hearts
   let us all check our hearts
       unto the Lord

we need Help.

the telling of secrets
05.25.2005, 10:07 p.m.

psst,
secrets
aren't hidden

your children
                      know them
your grandchildren
                      reveal them
maybe their children
                      will live them
           ...

                good or bad
                secrets
                          aren't really secrets.

Love loves loving

You named it Love
01.23.2005, 11:25 p.m.

      if a list
      i should write
      itemizing all
      the reasons why
      You couldn't
      possibly love
      me, it would go
      on and on:

1. i
2. can
3. think
4. of
5. quite
6. a
7. few
8. …

but You do.

pondering
how could You
possibly do it,
i am rendered
speechless:
      only One
      that outstretches
      infinity could
      possess such a
      truly indescribable

        Emotion
        Act
        Expression Experience,
        and form it into
        one word
        for my finite
        capabilities …

You called it love.

    and to be honest,
    it is too profound
    for me to capture:
        why would You have
        anything to do
        with me …

    but it's really true,
    all i know, Lord Jesus,
    is that You do …

and You named it love.

gettin' g'd up in Love, ya dig
fall 2006

feelin' my shorts
with a hot mill name
a new white-T, spankin'
another mill to the game
my wrinkle-free paid cash
oxford tag popped
and the rest
fresh
gear
Loves got on lock
my specs most aiight
sights me
Love mean and clean
my hat dons Love
max'd proper
hard cock'd—lean

it gots to be Love
you peep me in
from wrist to lobe
the froze fire within

breathe

how do i look
covered hard in it
add a swagger and
a smile
and get crunk-hyped
with it

if not
just worth a thin tin cymbal
ain't legit fake and phony
hard number one broken symbol

no doubt
representin'
i must labor in it

fresh start
strong heart
i'm a winner in it.

love?.
06.08.2005, 10:25 p.m.

do you love me
do you girl
do you
i know you
gots
love for me dawg
i know you do
boo you too
you love me
i know you do
pimp n
you gots to love me
you gots to
      now
i know
you love me ho   mie
no doubt you do
baby daddy
baby girl
baby sweet baby
me
do you love me
do you me
love me
do you …

                                            You love me
                                                 yes
                                    I AM loves me
                                             I AM
                                           loves
                                             me
                                  i am loving
                                              me.

#62
06.14.2005

You
require
love
like the Love
    that
love
i cannot
obtain
    by myself
even in
my thoughts
it is going
to take
all of You
to love You
like that Lord

and she
her beauti-
    ful
love-
    ly
    self
 needs
love
    which
i cannot
place
    in
    to
her hands
    as the gift
until
    You
    show me

how to
       love her
with the
            Love
that
must be acquired
from You,
the Beginning,
Lord.

the Love Gift
02.08.2005, 11:07 a.m.

flowers droop
        then wither
                and finally
                        life wanes
candies sit
      age
            turn rotten
                    and worm over
and decorated cards
      are hung high for display
                  then placed in a drawer

but long ago Lord,
possessing
no intent
of being disregarded
or hint of diminishing
or innateness of death,
    a Gift appeared
        Your Son, Jesus
        He is Your whole heart in flesh,

    the Valentine for the world.

just weather Friend
09.17.2006, 9:33 p.m.

    it was
sunny
    the entire week
her best friend
    passed on.

and for
twenty-four
    hours
it
rained
        when he took his wife—
            a God masterpiece.

and in
every
    moment
You, Lord,
are consistent
    as Friend and Lover.

Beloved
09.20.2004, 12:43 p.m.

for Kendrick and Sherrie Watson on 10.09.2004

My bride
the time has come to receive you—
And in this moment
when I reflect in you
all that I am,
which is all that I poured into you
all
that is lovely and pure
true
and everlasting
I say:
I love you.

Now, in this twinkling of an eye
as I receive a complete
yielding vessel
full of glory
overflowing with Myself
I say again:
I love you.

And in ages to come
like those past
I declare
to everything I deposited in you -
from one immeasurable distance
to another,
My words
like My heart
will not change:
I love you
I love you
I love you.

we are gathered here today
08.11.2006, 11:48 p.m.

> *for Wendell and Keisha Thompson on 08.19.2006*

directed as radiant light
you two meet
as cherished gifts
intended
      no known touch
intended
a pronouncement
of God's faithfulness
you are remnants of the masses
      many of your contemporaries
      are confounded
and as pure as the Father's thoughts
you are ordained
like the resplendent Life.
Selah

you may ask us
11.2006

    for Barraka and Lisa Nephilim on 11.25.2006

you may ask us

if we do know the feeling of touch
and if we are familiar with sensations

        yes, to both questions

but dwelling on the past
has never been good for us. ever.

and yes,
we are grateful for what
God has brought our way

and yes,
our hearts flutter when
     we see the gift of one another:

our actions tell it all.

we have never loved like this
this type of love is new to us

and yes, it was God's touch that saved us
and yes, it is God's familiar that sustains us

you may ask us.

    yes, i do
    love Him
    and her

        yes, i do
        love Him
        and him.

yes, i do.

The Messiah Gospel
01.27.2005

EAR:
        perfect Love makes us not ashamed
            It banishes all fear
      we open wide our mouths
            and proclaim It:
                  certainly convinced
                        of what It has done for us,
          It is real
    It has reached us and
          claimed us
                through It's power
and embraces us so dear.

EAR:
        perfect Love makes us not ashamed
        It banishes all fear.

worldwide

mined
fall 2006

you have a
      mine*d*
of
                                    diamonds *are forever*
within
      your grasp

      so plottin' on
                foreign lands
ain't necessary

            scheming *in* securities
                of others
ain't necessary

      flow the
deep
      ness of your
            own
      mine*d*

explore the potent
                        ial
      of your
            own
                God-given
                      prolifics

and stop

gettin' hustled
stop being
stopped
by kats
    doubting kats
        hating kats
    carnivorous kats
        feeding kats

"LOOOOOSERS"

    hustlers disguised as kats
        hustlin' you
for every
    red valued cent
of your
own
mine*d*.

kings and priests
c. 1992 - 1993

my son,
    do you not know that you were called to be
    royalty   regardless of the
curses that have flooded your ears

i know you weren't told that the true and living God
died for you out of love
to be His child
ordained
by Him   before the foundation of the world
    in Him
    in due of greatness
    in due   before you some how perish
    and become
no more   in barren lands
where there are
    no hints of summer   nor accepted laughter
    nor sounds of joyous celebration with your boys

my
    son,
    you are dying because you do not know that the King
of kings loves you.

my brother,
    i know you have become accustomed
to hearing the negative and searching and not finding the
positive

but during
        the inhaling and
                exhaling of wild trees
you cannot truly understand
that you should be reigning
sitting high
in heavenly places with Jesus, the Son
                        your thoughts have been so
                    clouded that
                        you don't know that your time is
                    drawing near for you to
accept Him
        and run
                and live
                      and run and love

        and run and give
true Life in this opportune time
before He withdraws His hand and
rejects
        you
                on the other side of creation
                        f   o   r   e   v   e   r

        where
                actualities
        of things you live/die for won't even exists

my
        brother,
stop
        giving heat like trivial opinions

        over young ladies with stylish weaves   or whatever
ignorant insignificant incidence
but wait, it is not too late
the time is now.

and my father
        during your heavy breathing belonging to
                a defiled ejaculation
                      and the knowledge of a planted seed

your time is at
        dawn
or perhaps at the cessation of your season
and   still   you have failed to learn
that you are called to be   priest of the Most High God
to represent heaven on earth and
                                      earth in
                            heaven

you are called to reflect the King of Glory in the earth
forever

you see in death
there will not be any hints
        or gradations of
                long fishing trips
                games of bones or
                the sound of melodic trumpets during the
        gentle caress of a woman's hands against your
unshaven face

today you somehow have misconstrued
being the head
as being
physically dominant over the woman that carries your
unborn child

men   this is the time
          during milky inhalation and whisky exhalation of
                thin new clouds and rusting skies

this is the time for you to let Jesus in your life and
          enlighten you about true love
                about manhood
and that you have been called out of
Elohim's Spirit to be more
to be kings and priests.

Revelation 1:6

worldwide
06.03.2005, 11:22 p.m.

there is this city
once a promise of
opportunity
a mecca
of vitality
now ruined by the self-
indulged
and a foresight
      that is
      behind-sight

an inner city.

a reflection of the
influentials'
intent-
      ional
inner-self
it is now being
abandoned
with broken windows
and sagging dreams
this city's name
is george

           and
                  there was this
                  subdivision
                  beautifully

                        planned with gorgeous
            views,
                    new
            school buildings and parks
                with blue water
                    fountains
                    a place of exact
                    precise
                    virtues. today it has
            been abused and mislead by the
                    administrators and their lies;
            sparse
                        now—it is corrupt and a
harbinger
                        to children of children chasing
                ecstasy like colorful dreams
                    at night
                    and we
                    named her
                    lailah

we named them
we named them all
    from this side
            to
            worldwide.
            they are
            our
                cities.
            we need
            to reclaim them

heal them
and rebuild them.
they must be
invested
in
for now and
generations
to come:

Isaiah 61:4.

this is only a test
06.03.2005, 11:22 p.m.

        Circle that which applies.

        my decision
        will affect

        my / his   seed in

        her / my   belly,

        its precious mind,
        its precious life
        and its precious

        child's mind and life.

        it might
        be the
        beginning of a vicious cycle
        so please,
        think it through.

dreamers
fall 2006

see
look around
everyone here
    is a dreamer
i am also
    a dreamer
    and i think,
        it is time to
    be about it

    see, if our creative
        visions
were placed
 in space
        they would
                          move
      as light.

    magnificent
        potential
            we have
but we dreamers
    are not exempt
here
of time and
        physical death
we are
within
two major

happenings
      every moment
           we move closer
           to the latter

look around
 we are all dreamers
                we are visionaries
     just like our Holy Creator

     it is really
time to be
         about it.

in october
06.03.2005, 7:40 p.m.

it is a cliché':
      the ice
      is fire
blah blah blah
blasé blasé blasé

but she really did
glow
when you placed
the rock
 on her finger

"i's married now," she exclaimed;
the SSD theory
          is really in motion
signed
sealed
delivered,
      she's yours

and now it seems
you own her
by being on her
with words
that batter hard like
a man's fist
and possibly
a fist will come
      but not from a *man*

partna,
you are breaking
her spirit
      dimming that glowing light

she is your wife
your beautiful
legacy
from the Lord.
     she is
          the mother of your legacy.
she is here
to help you
but how can
she help you
seeking help away
from you.

in season
fall 2006

sincere:
he does
what he knows
how to do
      more than anything
          he loves you
he is not your child
    nor a baby,
    but your husband.
         those word-tones are not
    for him.

 maybe
 perfection
is not near
    but effort
        and God
        are in his heart,
   truly.

for him are words like
    proper, respect

edify.

support child

support child
05.23.2005, 2:34 p.m.

before your strong
confident
yes
is
released,
baby
girl,
in all your love
you are not
enough
to be a father
      and when the checks
           arrive
on time
money will not
be able to
speak the Truth
as the man
can
to his child.

#48
05.22.2005, 9:34 p.m.

dear one

dear
young one,

wait
on right.

please

don'trushintowrong,

regret

is waiting there.

change; ex-currency
05.24.2005, 11:43 p.m.

when he told you that
you were a quarter
among dimes
you thought he
valued you
so you bought in
and gave it away
because of paltry words
when in Truth
you are a unique
coin
of astronomical worth
completely

tail
and
head.

investment
06.03.2005, 8:04 p.m.

hey
that coin you are,
take it
cherish it
add Jesus to it
invest it
and gain interest on it
multiply it with faith
and work it!

warning,
this is a warning:
06.03.2005, 8:18 p.m.

the tremors
are the sweet words
from the tightest
game
and your shaky yes
was a 9.5
on the Richter scale
it came out
of your diverse mouth
a deep fault
of the tongue
embedded in your spirit

now, that is
a sign of the times.

in this moment
08.11.2006, 10:22 p.m.

in that moment
you are
more than a
pre-mature yes
      to his wanting ear
you are a profound and
revealed no
a confident
      "i know who i am"

in this moment
in this
moment
in
this moment

tick-tock
tick-tock

in
this moment

you are a beautiful
divine purpose of God.

a healing start
08.01.2006

yes
i ran into her
the other day
and we had familiar conversations
about the old days.
it seemed like yesterday
that we graduated from
high school
matter of fact,
it was about two years ago
when we walked.

and we talked for a minute
and we laughed
so much that
my eyes watered
see, i've always been like that
laughing so hard, my eyes would water
but after a while
our talk became deep
and real
and she started crying
about some dude
she can't seem to cut loose
about some chump, that does her wrong
and she told me, just as soon as the tears
he made her cry dry,
there she goes running back to him.

she's hurting and she really doesn't know why.

call your daughter
call her
and love her
love her deeply
as God would you have.

even if she's not your seed.

selections

the hidden parts
06.14.2005, 4:38 p.m.

there is pain
deeply
and only you
know its force
so deep
not flesh owns it
but spirit;
    and
hard drinks
by the shot
enhance it
not wash it away
never drown it
    truly
or break it down
it cannot
reach it
to heal it
to salve it
but fester
it
fester sentiment
fester eyes
    brave mouth
fester soul
but there is
a Balm
with mighty Word
can reach it

pierce it
dissolve it
cover it
break it
    take your pick
and then
replace it
with Himself,
His whole saving Self.

Life
08.09.2006, 8:00 p.m.

it is night
and day is somewhere on
its way
but, Lord, Your spirit is here
and there
        It is a moving current
        forever flowing
        as fierce mighty wind
        and gentle as whispering love

You are always moving
connecting galaxies
and circling this living sphere
even into the center of our hearts

You are.

You move effortlessly
reaching the souls that have
been given up on
and touch them deep in
their bellies
        out reaching
        spreading diseases,
        planting eternal seeds
        into their dear children
        giving
        undeniable peace.

the Word saving
06.01.2005, 2:39 p.m.

Lord, Your word is
light unto itself
it came to
me in darkness
found me
out of void
it lead
me straight
surrounded me
pierced me
through all sides
and filled me
manifesting itself
to me
coming to live
with me
saving
my soul

it saved my life.

the potential
01.21.2005, 9:49 p.m.

in your spirit
      through My Spirit
           deeply
I have
      eyes
I want you to
look in
ears that want to
know the distinct tones of
your
                      voice
full

I have a voice
with a sound
ready
for your ears
only
      because
I am
God like that
      see   only you
can know Me as
      you can
look
      My heart
          is right here
              look closer if
          you are willing

and you will
          see there's a
deep
place here
just for
     you
eternally.

Your peace
12.27.2005, 5:53 p.m.

Jesus, i
discovered
Your peace
today
when i
talked
to You

in the stillness
of my spirit
and the
full joy
of what it
declared
a calmness
came
as if i was
floating
in
still
      a i r

a tranquility
came
upon me
like a gentle
kiss
abundant
with polite ness

with purity

and as i
submit to
You
i experience
Your peace and You
allow me to
travel in Your light
      like
      f l o w i n g water and
d
 anc
      ing
      wind.

a thread
01.24.2005, 10:55 p.m.

                    if
                  it's just
                a thread in
              the train of Your
        robe, Lord, i'll grab hold and won't let it go.

yes and amen
late summer 2001

Check this out:

He is
He be
He will
He did
He being
He is

Life in the fullest meaning

In His presence, He's satisfaction
at it's purest

In love, He's the true melodic *laaaaa*
the *aaaaah* in good
and *mmmmm* in so sweet

He done
He is
He does
He will do
He has
He is

     the Healer that makes you whole

In revelations, He's the Yah Yah Yah
the wow in amazing

and whoa in bad ...
      and I do mean mighty

As for sin, He overcame it when we were underneath it

He reigns supreme forever—the Eternal World Champion
                    our Champion ... He took on the world
and won ...

He encompasses the timeline of our being ...
                            the good and evil
                            the hero and the
villain
                            the saint and the
sinner

He's flowing red rivers of forgiveness
in yielding lands

Once again beloved,
      He's love ...
and if you just take a pause to think on Him ...

He's Jesus, our eternal prize...

He gon' do
He is
He done did

He has done
He is
He is doing

Has He?...
Is He gon' do?...
Will He?...
Is He?...
Did He?...
Is He gon' be?...

        Yes and amen.

me "church"
02.01.2005, 5:36 p.m.

me sunday
me church it
dress it up
praise it high:
        by and by
me sing through
and move too
me say amen

me check it
me sign it
me offer toward
me lay it *all?*
me say amen

me cried it
     tongue filled
me pray it again
     me shout till
me say no sin
me benedicted
me say amen

     me leave

     me week it
        work it
     me does what
        it pleases me

        me
        night it
            hide it
            and creep it
me sip it
    me taste it
    me peep it
    me kick it
        touch it
        me squeeze it
        me will
            feel it
    me say what me say
        when me say
        what me want to say
        how me say it
me say amen
        me do what me want
        when me want
        what me want
        if not, me won't
         or me may fight
                      you
me say me church
me said, me say me church
        and you bet not say me not

me sunday again
me say selah
me hallelujah
me say
no sin
me say amen.

sunday sounds
03.05.2005, 9:46 p.m.

sunday sounds
collective
voices
rising
higher and
higher
hymns lined
with winter fresh
scents
sunday sounds
deep tongues
bathing in breathing waters
baptismal splashing
sunday sounds
crackling cellophane wrappers
of sweet red and white
and
snapping tin of
cinnamon mints
sunday
sounds rattling
percussions
doom bop
tack t-tack
doom bop sound of suuuuuuuuuuun
day
instrumental winds
gliding and
floating
harmonies adoring
sailing
worshipping
sounds
high

praise
dance and
shout
shout
shouting sunday
sounds
fervent petitions and
clap
clap
clap of thankful hands
sunday sounds
sounds of sunday
Word forth
finding
piercing
healing sounds of sunday
wailing souls and
pouring hearts
joyous sounds
of sunday breakthrough
and deliverance
sounds
serenity of
God
peaceful
sounds of sunday.

and you know you should be singing
04.06.2005, 7:17 p.m.

there is fire
in your voice
put there by the Spirit of God
a consecrated sound
that doesn't need a
fire beat
it is so coated
with anointing
it possesses
an accompaniment
mysterious to gentiles
and uncircumcised ears

release it
to stop the enemy and
make him retreat

lives are dependent upon it.

come
09.20.2006, 9:25 p.m.

> *for Cecelia Jones*

come and
write
me your
vision
a rhyming cornucopia
of righteous living
        to set some dearth
        part of me free

come
        again,
illustrate
the sight
of your new mind
        and in my agreeing
spirit
        an explosion will
occur
as finale
fire works
against
night skies

        free
a dark part of me

to see
another
character-
 istic of the living God

write for me, please

write
for me.

write.

gifted
March 2002

for the Minors, with appreciation

gifted
so you're brilliant
take a pen, flip the script
paint a masterpiece, a vision
at worst, your expressions are prolific
you dance like birds in full motion
sing like angels' voices
play like three hands
gifted
gift ed.
can it transform,
survive the test of fire
is it from Jesus, your vision
that classic you wrote, is it eternal
singing: does it serve like angels
will give-ted seeds give life
or will death come
gift ed.

the Truth is the Truth
06.01.2005, 2:48 p.m.

regardless
of being
alone
in a room
laughing fully
or deeply sobbing

and regardless
of whispering
in a crowd
at an amusement park or
intellectualizing
a conversation
inside a lobby
of a cinema

and regardless
of being deep
in love
or warring
lust,
i have come
to realize:
Truth

this can be
a poem or
prose or just
rambling of words
but nonetheless, Lord,
Your word is Truth
forever and ever
amen.

The Empty Tomb

The Empty Tomb
01.05.2005

In your philosophy,
what profound ending are you
grasping for?

                                      What reasoning has you clueless?

            Which
       deception has
      been tried and
        true? Which
        temptation is
          made of
           pure
           gold?

                                    What rationale has you exalted?

Please explain, what god is there in a filled tomb? Is there
no answer in a filled tomb, except death?

With your
tongue, what
manipulation
are you
formulating?
In your
mind, what
formulation are
you calculating?
In your heart,
what deviation
are you
deviating?

                              Tell me, what new schism
                              are you scheming?

                              What lie has you
                              believing a lie? Isn't
                              the Creator the
                              Truth, regardless
                              of a
                              false witness
                              (deceiver),
                              because the
                              witness is
                              really
                              false?

And the things the Creator says,
aren't they the Truth;
and we can ask Him
for
ourselves?

                              Why seek
                              the closed
                              tomb when
                              the stone was
                              rolled away?

The questions are the questions, but the answer, is the
Answer.

Before there was a beginning and an ending, the Lord spoke it to be, simultaneously. He reached into time and created. The solar systems are mist from His mouth; the universes are set by His boundaries. The sun is a sparkle in His eye; the moon, just a speck. It is He that separated heaven from earth and spiritual from natural. He called beings and miraculously gave them life.

It is He that proclaimed "I am that I am." And because there was no other way, He humbled Himself in human form and called Him Jesus. Yes Jesus, submitted Himself to His will because He is the only way. He died as He said He would and was raised just as He said, with all power in His hands—life and death included. It is He that ascended into Heaven to prepare a place and is now sitting at the right hand of the Father—reigning with the Father. And in the end, He shall return in all of His marvelous glory!

Why seek a filled tomb, when it is empty?